donna hay

SIMPLE ESSENTIALS

christmas

thank you

Seeing as Christmas is the season of giving, I'm going to take this opportunity to thank a few of the people who have given their time and talent to this little book, which started life as a breezy idea of mine one morning and ended up taking over all our lives for several weeks. Self indulgent? Maybe, but here goes. First my right-hand man, Con Poulos, and his fellow photographers Chris Court and Ben Dearnley, who made the food look so beautiful and gave my recipes life. Next, my designer, Ann Gordon, who took a jumble of words and pictures and turned them into something that looks as if it was planned this way all along. I couldn't have coped without the fantastic ideas and sheer hard work of my food editors, Justine Poole and Steve Pearce, recipe tester Tom Frawley, and merchandiser/stylist Lucy Weight, who gathered together all those little props that make each image so special. At the business end I have to thank my editor, Sara Mulcahy, who never once lost her Christmas spirit (that's quite an achievement in the middle of June) and my copy editor, Abi Weeks, who patiently weeded out all my 'donna-isms' and made this book a joy to read as well as look at. And of course Gary Woodside and his trusty production team, and Paul at Graphic Print Group who ensured everything looks as good on the page as it did when it came out of the oven. Finally (I promise) special thanks go to my partner Bill, my sons Angus and Tom, and the rest of my family who always make Christmas so… eventful. Cheers.

on the cover

Sparkly festive biscuits. Follow the recipe for vanilla snap biscuits on page 46. Cut out the biscuits in your preferred shapes, use a skewer to pierce a hole for the ribbon and sprinkle with sanding sugar before baking.

Fourth Estate

An imprint of HarperCollins*Publishers*

First edition published in Australia, New Zealand and Canada in 2005, by Fourth Estate, an imprint of HarperCollins*Publishers*
This edition published in 2007
HarperCollins*Publishers* Australia Pty Limited
Level 13, 201 Elizabeth Street, Sydney, NSW 2000, Australia
ABN 36 009 913 517

DONNA HAY CHRISTMAS Copyright © Donna Hay 2005, 2007
Design copyright © Donna Hay 2005, 2007
Photographs copyright © Con Poulos 2005 cover, pages 1, 4, 7, 9, 11–13, 15–17, 19, 21–23, 25, 30–43, 45, 47–49, 53–63, 80; © Chris Court pages 11, 12, 29, 64; © Ben Dearnley pages 21, 27; © William Meppem 42, 51 © Lisa Cohen 47.

Art Direction: Ann Gordon
Editor: Sara Mulcahy
Copy Editor: Abi Weeks
Food Editors: Justine Poole, Steve Pearce, Tom Frawley
Merchandising: Lucy Weight

Produced in China by RR Donnelley on 157gsm Chinese Matt Art

National Library of Australia Cataloguing-in-Publication data:

Hay, Donna.
Simple essentials : Christmas / Donna Hay
ISBN 978 0 7322 8718 4 (hbk.)
Simple essentials
Includes index.
Christmas cookery.
641.5686

16 / 14 13 12 11

donna hay

SIMPLE ESSENTIALS

christmas

FOURTH ESTATE

contents

introduction

We all look forward to this special time of year. It's about family, friends, gifts, parties… and food, which is where that vaguely uneasy feeling can start to set in. So that's why I've compiled this book. There's a traditional menu with turkey, a collection of simple recipes for the time-poor and a chapter on sweet treats laden with goodies to enjoy throughout the season. I've also included menu planners to ensure you spend minimal time in the kitchen and a section on decorating your home. So whatever kind of festive season you're anticipating, there's something to suit. Welcome to your most fuss-free Christmas ever.

Donna

traditional christmas

If you're hosting the family Christmas, take inspiration
from your grandmother's kitchen for these festive classics.
And remember, many hands make light work.

NIBBLES

chilli spiced nuts ✳ saffron risotto cakes
✳ chive frittatas with smoked salmon
✳ thyme and brandy pâté

MAINS

perfect roasted turkey ✳ roast pork loin
✳ glazed ham

SIDES

honey and spice glazed vegetables
garlic roast asparagus ✳ red onion and potato gratin
✳ peas with pancetta and mint

DESSERTS

christmas pudding ✳ grandma's fruit cake
✳ brandy and vanilla custard

combined menu serves 12–16

saffron risotto cakes

1 pinch saffron threads
2 tablespoons boiling water
1 quantity basic risotto (recipe, page 76), chilled
50g (1¾ oz) mozzarella, cut into 16 pieces
vegetable oil for shallow-frying

Place the saffron threads in a heatproof bowl, pour over the boiling water and set aside for 10 minutes. Add the saffron threads and liquid to the risotto and mix to combine. Take a heaped tablespoonful of risotto and mould it in the palm of your hand. Place a piece of mozzarella in the middle and press the risotto over to enclose, shaping it into a cake. Repeat with the remaining mixture. Refrigerate the risotto cakes until needed. Heat the oil in a saucepan over medium heat. When oil is hot, shallow-fry the cakes for 2–3 minutes or until golden. Drain on absorbent paper. Makes 16.

chive frittatas with smoked salmon

6 eggs
1 cup (8 fl oz) (single or pouring) cream
¾ cup grated cheddar cheese
2 tablespoons chopped chives
sea salt and cracked black pepper
topping
½ cup sour cream
80g (2¾ oz) cream cheese, softened
1½ tablespoons lemon juice
50g (1¾ oz) sliced smoked salmon
snipped chives, extra, to garnish

Preheat oven to 160°C (320°F). Place the eggs, cream, cheddar, chives, salt and pepper in a bowl and mix to combine. Pour into 12 x ½ cup (4 fl oz) capacity greased muffin tins and bake for 15 minutes or until set. Remove from the tins and cool slightly. To serve, combine the sour cream, cream cheese and lemon juice in a bowl and place a teaspoonful on top of each frittata. Top with a small piece of smoked salmon and garnish with the extra chives. Makes 12.

thyme and brandy pâté

20g (¾ oz) butter
2 teaspoons olive oil
2 small brown onions, chopped
2 cloves garlic, crushed
4 teaspoons thyme leaves
600g (1⅓ lb) chicken livers, trimmed
4 tablespoons brandy
100g (3½ oz) butter, extra, softened
⅔ cup (5 fl oz) (single or pouring) cream
sea salt and cracked black pepper
1 cup (8 fl oz) canned chicken consommé
2 teaspoons gelatine powder
¼ cup juniper berries

Heat a large non-stick frying pan over medium heat. Add the butter, oil, onions, garlic and thyme and cook for 1 minute or until soft. Add the livers and cook for a further minute. Pour in the brandy and cook until evaporated. Process the liver mixture with the extra butter and the cream until smooth. Season well with salt and pepper. Push the mixture through a sieve and spoon into 8 x ½ cup (4 fl oz) capacity dishes. In a small pan, warm the consommé over low heat. Add the gelatine and stir until dissolved. Allow to cool slightly. Place a few juniper berries on each pâté and pour in the consommé to fill the dishes. Refrigerate until firm. Makes 8.

chilli spiced nuts

2 tablespoons vegetable or peanut oil
2 teaspoons mild ground chilli
4 teaspoons smoky sweet paprika
2 teaspoons sea salt
2 teaspoons ground cumin
3 cups mixed nuts of your choice

Heat a frying pan over medium–high heat. Add the oil, chilli, paprika, salt and cumin and stir for 2 minutes or until the spices are fragrant. Add the nuts and stir for 5 minutes or until the nuts are golden. Makes 3 cups.

saffron risotto cakes

thyme and brandy pâté

chive frittatas with smoked salmon

chilli spiced nuts

11

perfect roasted turkey

roast pork loin

glazed ham

13

perfect roasted turkey

3kg (6½ lb) turkey
60g (2 oz) butter
2 quantities stuffing (for stuffing recipes, see pages 16 and 17)
vegetable oil, for brushing
1½ cups (12 fl oz) chicken stock

Preheat the oven to 180°C (355°F). Wash the turkey, pat dry and tuck the wings underneath. Gently push a spoon between the skin of the turkey and the breast meat to release the skin from the flesh (take care not to split the skin). Using your fingers, evenly distribute the butter under the skin. Loosely fill the turkey cavity with stuffing. Close the cavity with a thin metal skewer and secure the legs with kitchen string. Lightly brush the turkey with the oil and place on a greased rack in a baking dish filled with the stock. Cover with greased aluminium foil and roast for 1 hour 30 minutes. Remove the foil and cook for a further 30 minutes or until the skin is golden and the turkey is cooked when tested with a skewer. Rest the turkey for 20 minutes before carving. Serves 6.

roast pork loin

2kg (4½ lb) loin of pork
2 quantities stuffing (for stuffing recipes, see pages 16 and 17)
vegetable oil, for rubbing
sea salt
10 small apples

Preheat the oven to 220°C (425°F). With the point of a sharp knife, score the skin of the pork at 1.5cm (⅔ in) intervals. Lay the loin out flat, place the stuffing down the middle and roll up. Secure with kitchen string and rub the skin with the oil and salt. Place the meat on a rack in a baking dish. Bake for 30 minutes. Reduce the heat to 200°C (390°F) and bake for a further 30 minutes. Make a cut around the circumference of the apples, place with the pork on the baking rack and cook for a further 20 minutes or until the pork is cooked to your liking. Slice and serve with the apples. Serves 6–8.

glazed ham

8kg (18 lb) leg ham
cloves, for studding
glaze
½ cup (4 fl oz) fresh orange juice
⅓ cup brown sugar
¼ cup dijon mustard
⅓ cup (2½ fl oz) honey

Preheat the oven to 190°C (375°F). Remove the skin from the ham and discard. Score the fat in a diamond pattern (see glossary). Stud a clove in the middle of each diamond. Place the ham in a baking dish lined with a few layers of non-stick baking (parchment) paper.

To make the glaze, place the orange juice, sugar, mustard and honey in a small saucepan over medium heat. Simmer, stirring occasionally, for 15 minutes or until thickened. Brush the ham with the glaze and bake for 10 minutes. Glaze again and bake for another 10 minutes. Repeat and bake for a final 10 minutes or until golden. Allow the ham to stand for 5 minutes before carving. Serves 10–12.

perfectly cooked pork

+ **timing is everything** It isn't necessary to cook pork until it is completely dried out, as was the fashion in the past. (According to an old wives' tale, overcooking pork guarded against disease.) Try cooking your pork to medium rather than well done and taste the difference.

+ **complementary flavours** Pork goes well with many flavours; apple and herbs (such as sage, parsley, thyme and rosemary) can be placed under the pork before baking or incorporated into the stuffing.

+ For more tips on cooking pork, see page 38.

couscous stuffing

Combine 1 cup couscous with 1¼ cups (10 fl oz) boiling chicken or vegetable stock. Cover and stand until the stock is absorbed. Add ¼ cup chopped fresh herbs (such as parsley, basil, chives, thyme or rosemary), 2 chopped cooked onions or leeks and cracked black pepper and sea salt and mix well. Use for meat or fish.

lemon and herb stuffing

Mix 3 cups fresh breadcrumbs with 2 teaspoons finely grated lemon rind, ¼ cup chopped mixed fresh herbs (such as parsley, basil, thyme, rosemary or chives), 60g (2 oz) soft butter, sea salt and cracked black pepper. Use for chicken, veal or lamb; double the quantities for a turkey.

caramelised onion stuffing

Cook 1 tablespoon olive oil, 1 tablespoon butter and 4 sliced red onions in a small pan over low heat for 10 minutes or until the onions are soft and golden. Add 3–4 cups fresh breadcrumbs and 1 tablespoon chopped herbs (sage, thyme, oregano or rosemary) and mix well. Use for beef, veal, lamb or chicken.

easy herb stuffing

Cook 2 teaspoons olive oil and 1 finely chopped onion in a frying pan over medium–high heat for 5 minutes. In a large bowl combine the onion, 3 cups fresh white breadcrumbs, 1½ teaspoons dried mixed herbs, 30g (1 oz) soft butter, sea salt and cracked black pepper and mix well. Use for chicken or lamb; double the quantities for a turkey.

white wine and thyme mustard

2 tablespoons black or brown mustard seeds
6 tablespoons yellow mustard seeds
⅓ cup (2½ fl oz) white wine vinegar
⅓ cup (2½ fl oz) chardonnay
¼ cup (2 fl oz) honey
1 tablespoon lemon juice
1 teaspoon lemon thyme leaves
sea salt and cracked black pepper

Place the mustard seeds in a non-metallic bowl and pour over the vinegar and wine. Cover and stand overnight. Place the mustard seed mixture in a small food processor or mortar and pestle with the honey, lemon juice, thyme, salt and pepper. Grind the mixture until almost smooth. Spoon into a hot sterilised jar and seal. Allow to cool and store in the refrigerator for up to 1 week. Makes approximately 1 cup (8 fl oz).

cheat's cranberry sauce

500g (1 lb) frozen cranberries
2 cups caster (superfine) sugar
¼ cup (2 fl oz) malt vinegar
¼ cup (2 fl oz) port

Preheat the oven to 200°C (390°F). Place the cranberries in a baking dish, add the sugar, vinegar and port and toss well to combine. Cook for 30 minutes or until the cranberries are soft and the sauce is thickened. Spoon into hot sterilised jars and store in the fridge for up to 2 weeks. Serve warm or cold with roast turkey or pork. Makes 3 cups (24 fl oz).

beetroot and balsamic relish

750g (1½ lb) beetroot, peeled and coarsely grated
1 brown onion, finely chopped
2 cups (16 fl oz) balsamic vinegar
1 cup (8 fl oz) water
3 teaspoons yellow mustard seeds
2½ cups granulated sugar
2 cloves
5cm (2 in) piece orange rind
sea salt and cracked black pepper

Place the beetroot, onion, vinegar, water, mustard seeds, sugar, cloves, orange rind, salt and pepper in a large, deep frying pan or jam pan. Place over medium heat, cover and bring to the boil. Cook for 30 minutes or until the beetroot is soft and the liquid has reduced and thickened slightly. Spoon into hot sterilised jars and seal. Allow to cool and store in the fridge for up to 2 months. Makes 5 cups (2 pints).

basic gravy

pan juices from roast chicken, turkey, lamb, beef or pork
10–12 ice cubes
2½ tablespoons plain (all-purpose) flour
stock, wine or water, to add to pan juices

Remove the roasted meat or poultry from the baking dish and keep warm. Pour the pan juices into a jug with the ice cubes and allow the fat to solidify. Skim off and reserve 2 tablespoons of the solidified fat, discard the remaining fat, reserving the pan juices. Return the reserved fat to the baking dish, add the flour to the fat in the baking dish and stir over medium heat for 4–5 minutes or until the paste is a light golden colour. Make the pan juices in the jug up to 2 cups (16 fl oz) with the stock, wine or water. Slowly whisk the liquid into the flour mixture until a smooth consistency. Stir over medium heat until the gravy comes to the boil and thickens. Makes 2 cups (16 fl oz).

white wine and thyme mustard

beetroot and balsamic relish

cheat's cranberry sauce

basic gravy

garlic roast asparagus

2–3 bunches asparagus, trimmed
olive oil
4 cloves garlic, sliced
shredded rind of 1 lemon
lemon juice, to serve
shaved parmesan cheese, to serve

Preheat the oven to 180°C (355°F). Place the asparagus in a baking dish. Sprinkle over a generous amount of olive oil and toss with the garlic and lemon rind. Cover and bake for 25–35 minutes or until the asparagus is tender. Serve with a squeeze of lemon and the shaved parmesan. Serves 8.

honey and spice glazed vegetables

1kg (2¼ lb) butternut pumpkin, cut into wedges
1kg (2¼ lb) sweet potato, peeled and quartered
4 parsnips, peeled and halved
2 celeriac (celery root), peeled and quartered
2–3 tablespoons vegetable oil
honey and spice glaze
½ cup (4 fl oz) honey, warmed
1 teaspoon ground chilli
1 teaspoon ground sweet paprika
1 teaspoon ground cumin
1 teaspoon ground coriander (cilantro)
sea salt and cracked black pepper

Preheat oven to 180°C (355°F). Place the vegetables into 2 baking dishes lined with non-stick baking (parchment) paper. Toss the vegetables with the oil and bake for 45 minutes or until just tender. To make the honey and spice glaze, mix together the honey, chilli, paprika, cumin, coriander, salt and pepper. Brush generously over the vegetables and bake for a further 10 minutes or until the vegetables are golden. Serves 8.

red onion and potato gratin

8 desiree potatoes, thinly sliced
4 red onions, thinly sliced
1 tablespoon thyme leaves
1 cup finely grated parmesan cheese
sea salt and cracked black pepper
1 cup (8 fl oz) (single or pouring) cream
½ cup (4 fl oz) beef or vegetable stock

Preheat the oven to 200°C (390°F). Place a layer of potato in the bases of two 1 litre (32 fl oz) capacity ovenproof dishes. Top with a third of the onion, thyme, parmesan, salt and pepper. Repeat with the remaining ingredients, finishing with a layer of potato. Top with any remaining parmesan and thyme. Combine the cream and stock in a bowl and pour over the layered potato. Cover the dishes with foil, place on a baking tray and bake for 20 minutes. Remove the foil and cook for a further 30 minutes or until the potato is tender and the top is golden. Serves 8.

peas with pancetta and mint

½ cup (4 fl oz) chicken stock
5 cups fresh or frozen peas (2kg/4½ lb in the pod)
12 slices pancetta, chopped
60g (2 oz) butter
¼ cup shredded mint leaves
cracked black pepper

Bring the stock to the boil in a saucepan over medium–high heat. Add the peas, cover and cook for 5 minutes or until tender. Meanwhile, place the pancetta in a frying pan over high heat and stir for 2 minutes or until crisp. Toss the pancetta, butter, mint and pepper with the peas and serve immediately. Serves 8.

garlic roast asparagus

red onion and potato gratin

honey and spice glazed vegetables

peas with pancetta and mint

21

christmas pudding   brandy and vanilla custard

grandma's fruit cake

christmas pudding

¾ cup sultanas

1 cup currants

1½ cups raisins, halved

¾ cup chopped pitted prunes or dates

⅔ cup candied mixed peel

⅔ cup slivered almonds

½ cup (4 fl oz) brandy or sherry

250g (8¾ oz) butter, softened

¼ cup brown sugar

¼ cup granulated sugar

3 eggs

1 cup plain (all-purpose) flour, sifted

1 teaspoon ground cinnamon

1 teaspoon mixed spice

250g (8¾ oz) fresh breadcrumbs

⅔ cup (5 fl oz) milk

1 x 80cm (30 in) square of calico cloth (see glossary)

plain (all-purpose) flour, extra

Place the sultanas, currants, raisins, prunes, mixed peel, almonds and brandy in a bowl and allow to soak for at least 4 hours. Place the butter, brown sugar and sugar in the bowl of an electric mixer and beat until light and creamy. Gradually add the eggs and beat well. Transfer the butter mixture to a large bowl. Add the fruit mixture, flour, cinnamon, mixed spice, breadcrumbs and milk and mix with a wooden spoon until well combined. Wearing rubber gloves, dip the calico in boiling water and carefully squeeze to remove any excess water. While the cloth is still hot, rub in the extra flour to form a skin around the pudding. Place the fruit mixture in the middle and gather up the ends of the cloth firmly around it. Tie the cloth with kitchen string as close to the mixture as possible, making a loop at the end of the string. Place the pudding in a saucepan of boiling water and boil for 4 hours 30 minutes, adding more water if necessary. Remove the pudding from the pan and hang on a broomstick over a sink. Allow to cool. Store in the fridge for up to 2 months. To reheat, boil for 45 minutes and drain for 5 minutes. Unwrap and serve with brandy and vanilla custard (right) or brandy butter (see page 50). Serves 12.

brandy and vanilla custard

2 tablespoons cornflour (cornstarch)

3 cups (24 fl oz) (single or pouring) cream

¼ cup (2 fl oz) brandy

1 split, scraped vanilla bean (see glossary)

6 egg yolks

⅓ cup caster (superfine) sugar

Mix the cornflour with a little of the cream until smooth. Set aside. Heat the cream, brandy and vanilla bean and seeds in a pan over medium heat until warm. Whisk together the yolks and sugar. Remove the vanilla bean and slowly whisk the egg and the cornflour mixtures into the cream mixture. Stir over low heat for 4 minutes or until thick. Makes 3½ cups (28 fl oz).

grandma's fruit cake

3 cups raisins

1½ cups sultanas

1 cup currants

¾ cup chopped dates

1 cup slivered almonds

¾ cup (6 fl oz) brandy

250g (8¾ oz) butter, softened

1¼ cups brown sugar

4 eggs

2¼ cups plain (all-purpose) flour, sifted

¼ teaspoon bicarbonate of soda (baking soda)

1 teaspoon ground cinnamon

2–3 tablespoons brandy, extra

Place the fruit and nuts in a bowl and pour over the brandy. Cover and allow to soak overnight. Preheat the oven to 140°C (285°F). Place the butter and sugar in the bowl of an electric mixer and beat until light and creamy. Gradually add the eggs and beat well. Place the butter and fruit mixtures, flour, bicarbonate of soda and cinnamon in a bowl and stir to combine. Line a 20cm (8 in) square cake tin with two layers of non-stick baking (parchment) paper. Spoon in the mixture and bake for 2 hours or until cooked. Pour over the extra brandy while the cake is hot. Cool in the tin. Serves 12.

traditional menu: planning ahead

up to 2 months before

☐ Make the Christmas pudding, wrap tightly in plastic wrap and store in the refrigerator.

☐ Make the fruit cake, store in an airtight container or wrapped in plastic wrap in a cake tin. Keep in a cool place.

3–4 weeks before

☐ Order the turkey, pork and ham and arrange a time and date for collection.

☐ Make the white wine and thyme mustard and store in an airtight container in the refrigerator.

2 weeks before

☐ Make the cheat's cranberry sauce and store in the refrigerator.

☐ Make the ham glaze and store in the refrigerator.

☐ Make the beetroot and balsamic relish and store in the refrigerator.

1 week before

☐ Decide on and purchase the wines, aperitifs, beers and soft drinks to go with your menu.

3 days before

☐ Purchase all remaining fresh fruit and vegetables required for your menu.

☐ Choose your stuffings for the turkey and pork, prepare and refrigerate until required. Don't stuff the pork or turkey until the day you are cooking it.

2 days before

☐ Make the saffron risotto cakes and refrigerate until ready to cook. You can also cook these ahead of time and reheat, covered, in a warm oven or microwave.

☐ Make the thyme and brandy pâté, cover and refrigerate. Stand at room temperature for 10 minutes before serving.

1 day before

☐ Make the red onion and potato gratin and refrigerate until required. Reheat covered with aluminium foil.

☐ Cook the chilli spiced nuts. Store in an airtight container. Before serving, warm in the microwave for 20–30 seconds.

☐ Glaze and cook the ham as you probably won't have room in the oven on the day. Reheat the ham on the day in a 190°C (375°F) oven for 20 minutes.

on the day

☐ Prepare the turkey and pork, fill with the stuffings and place on baking dishes to roast.

+ turkey cooking guide
20 minutes at 180°C (355°F) per 500g (1 lb)
To ensure a perfectly roasted turkey, cook it covered for most of the oven time to keep the outer parts from becoming dry. Remove the cover in the last 30 minutes to brown and crisp up the skin. Alternatively, place some softened butter between the skin and the breast to keep the meat moist.

☐ Cook the chive frittatas and store at room temperature. Add the cream cheese and smoked salmon just before serving.

☐ Cook the garlic roast asparagus and store in the refrigerator. Reheat, covered, in a hot oven or microwave or serve at room temperature.

☐ Place the turkey in the oven 2½ hours before serving.

☐ Place the pork in the oven 1½ hours before serving.

☐ Place the honey and spice glazed vegetables in the oven 45 minutes before serving. If you are short of oven space, use the smallest oven trays you have and place things side by side. Alternatively, cook the vegetables in a covered barbecue outside.

☐ Make the brandy and vanilla custard, cover and keep warm until required.

☐ Cook the peas with pancetta and mint and keep covered with the saucepan lid to keep the peas warm.

☐ Make the gravy, pour into a jug. Cover and keep warm until required.

☐ Before sitting down to eat, place the Christmas pudding in a large saucepan of boiling water for 45 minutes to reheat.

tips + tricks

+ **will the turkey fit in the oven?** If you're not sure, measure the space from the bottom shelf to the top of the oven and the baking dish before you go shopping. Take these measurements and a tape measure to the butcher's or supermarket; you might look strange measuring up a turkey, but it'll save worse embarrassment on Christmas day. An alternative is to cook the turkey in a covered barbecue, or buy boneless turkey breasts that will fit on a baking tray.

+ **not enough space in your oven?** You can cook the turkey the day before and serve it cold. Cook the pork and vegetables on the day and serve them hot. Don't reheat cooked turkey or pork, as it will dry out. And don't partially cook meat or poultry or you risk bacterial contamination. Vegetables that take an hour or so to cook can be roasted ahead of time and reheated later.

simple christmas

Being short on time doesn't mean you have to compromise on flavour or style. This fuss-free menu will ensure that your easiest Christmas ever is also one of your best.

NIBBLES

flavoured olives ✻ goat's cheese and dill quiches

STARTER

✻ salmon and rocket tarts

MAIN

✻ roast pork rack with apples and sage

SIDES

green bean and broccolini balsamic salad

mustard cream ✻ muffin stuffing

✻ crunchy baby potatoes

DESSERTS

chocolate christmas pudding

✻ honey and nutmeg biscuits

combined menu serves 8

goat's cheese and dill quiches

flavoured olives

salmon and rocket tarts

goat's cheese and dill quiches

3 sheets store-bought shortcrust pastry or 600g (1⅓ lb)
    shortcrust pastry (recipe, page 76)
filling
80g (2¾ oz) goat's cheese
¼ cup dill sprigs
4 egg yolks
1⅓ cups (10½ fl oz) (single or pouring) cream
½ teaspoon finely grated lemon rind
sea salt and cracked black pepper

Preheat the oven to 160°C (320°F). Cut each pastry sheet into
4 squares. On a baking tray lined with non-stick baking (parchment)
paper, line 12 greased egg rings with the pastry and trim any excess.
Place the goat's cheese and dill in the cases. Whisk the egg yolks,
cream, lemon rind, salt and pepper. Pour the egg mixture into the
cases. Bake for 30 minutes or until the top is golden and the filling
is set. Remove the egg rings to serve. Makes 12.

flavoured olives

250g (8¾ oz) kalamata olives
250g (8¾ oz) green olives
1 tablespoon shredded lemon rind
1 tablespoon thyme leaves
1 teaspoon cracked black pepper
¼ cup (2 fl oz) lemon juice
2 large red chillies, chopped
2 tablespoons olive oil

Combine the olives, lemon rind, thyme, pepper, lemon juice, chilli and
olive oil. Allow to marinate for at least 4 hours or preferably overnight.
Store in an airtight container in the refrigerator for up to 1 week. Serve
with pre-dinner drinks. Serves 8.

salmon and rocket tarts

1 sheet store-bought butter puff pastry, defrosted
1 egg, lightly beaten
¾ cup sour cream
2 teaspoons white wine vinegar
1 tablespoon chopped tarragon leaves
1 green onion (scallion), chopped
1 tablespoon salted capers, rinsed and drained
sea salt and cracked black pepper
1 bunch (100g/3½ oz) rocket
8 slices smoked salmon

Preheat the oven to 200°C (390°F). Cut the pastry sheet into 4 x 6cm
(2⅓ in) squares. Cut each piece in half, place on a baking tray lined
with baking paper and brush with the egg. Bake in the oven for
10 minutes or until puffed and golden. Place the sour cream, vinegar,
tarragon, green onion, capers, salt and pepper in a bowl and stir to
combine. Spoon the sour cream mixture onto the tarts and top with
the rocket and salmon to serve. Makes 8.

roast pork rack with apples and sage

2kg (4½ lb) pork rack (10 cutlets), with skin on
¼ cup (2 fl oz) olive oil
sea salt
4 green apples, cored and quartered
2 tablespoons sage leaves
2 tablespoons lemon juice
2 tablespoons brown sugar

Preheat the oven to 220°C (425°F). Use a sharp knife to score the
pork skin at small intervals. Rub the pork generously with the oil and
salt. Place the pork on a rack in a baking dish and roast for 30 minutes
or until the skin starts to crackle. Reduce the temperature to 200°C
(390°F) and roast for a further 25 minutes. Place the apples, sage,
lemon juice and sugar in a bowl and toss to combine. Add the apples
to the baking dish and roast with the pork for a further 25 minutes or
until the pork is cooked through and the apples are tender. Serves 8.

roast pork rack with apples and sage

mustard cream

300g (10½ oz) sour cream
⅓ cup seeded mustard
2 teaspoons finely grated lemon rind
sea salt and cracked black pepper

Place the sour cream, mustard, lemon rind, salt and pepper in a bowl and mix to combine. Refrigerate until required. Serves 8.

crunchy baby potatoes

32 baby/chat (new) potatoes
⅓ cup (2½ fl oz) olive oil
sea salt and cracked black pepper

Preheat the oven to 200°C (400°F). Use a small sharp knife to cut thin slices into the potato, ensuring you don't cut all the way through. Place the potatoes in a bowl with the oil, salt and pepper and toss to coat. Place in a baking dish and roast for 35–40 minutes or until golden and crunchy. Serves 8.

green bean and broccolini balsamic salad

300g (10½ oz) green beans, trimmed and blanched
2 bunches (180g) broccollini, trimmed and blanched
bacon balsamic dressing
50g (1¾ oz) butter
¼ cup (2 fl oz) olive oil
2 eschalots, chopped
3 rashers bacon, trimmed and chopped
⅓ cup (2½ fl oz) lemon juice
1 tablespoon balsamic vinegar
sea salt and cracked black pepper

To make the bacon balsamic dressing, place the butter and oil in a medium non-stick frying pan over medium heat and stir until the butter is melted. Add the eschalots and bacon and cook for 5–7 minutes or until the bacon is golden. Add the lemon juice, vinegar, salt and pepper and cook for a further minute. Add the beans and broccolini and cook for 2–3 minutes or until warmed through. Serves 8.

muffin stuffing

100g (3½ oz) butter
1 brown onion, sliced
2 cloves garlic, crushed
2 tablespoons finely grated lemon rind
⅓ cup chopped chives
½ cup chopped flat-leaf parsley leaves
1 tablespoon chopped sage leaves
1 loaf white bread, crusts removed and roughly torn
2 eggs, lightly beaten

Preheat the oven to 200°C (390°F). Heat a large non-stick frying pan over high heat. Add the butter, onion, garlic and lemon rind and cook for 3–4 minutes or until the onions are tender. Add the chives, parsley, sage and bread. Cook for 1 minute. Remove from the heat and stir in the eggs. Spoon the mixture into 12 x ½ cup (4 fl oz) capacity greased muffin tins and bake for 15 minutes or until golden. Makes 12.

mustard cream

green bean and broccolini balsamic salad

crunchy baby potatoes

muffin stuffing

chocolate christmas pudding

1 cup dried dates
1 teaspoon bicarbonate of soda (baking soda)
¾ cup (6 fl oz) boiling water
55g (2 oz) unsalted butter, softened
1 teaspoon vanilla extract
¾ cup (5½ oz) brown sugar
4 eggs
¾ cup (4½ oz) self-raising (self-rising) flour, sifted
¼ cup (1¼ oz) cocoa powder, sifted
100g (3½ oz) dark chocolate, melted
chocolate brandy sauce
¾ cup (6 fl oz) (single or pouring) cream
⅓ cup (2⅔ oz) brown sugar
200g (7 oz) dark chocolate, chopped
25g (¾ oz) unsalted butter
1 tablespoon brandy

To make the chocolate brandy sauce, place the cream, sugar, chocolate and butter in a small saucepan over low heat and stir for 5–6 minutes or until the mixture is smooth. Stir in the brandy and set aside.

Place the dates, bicarbonate of soda and water in a bowl and stand for 10–15 minutes. Blend or process the date mixture until smooth and set aside. Place the butter, vanilla and sugar in an electric mixer and beat for 10–12 minutes or until well combined. Add the eggs, one at a time, beating well after each addition. Add the flour, cocoa, chocolate and the date mixture and beat well. Spoon into a lightly greased 7-cup capacity pudding basin, cover and secure with string. Place the pudding in a large saucepan and fill with boiling water to come ¾ up the side of the basin. Cook for 2 hours 45 minutes, adding more water as necessary. Remove from the saucepan, stand for 10–15 minutes and turn out. Serve with chocolate brandy sauce. Serves 8.

honey and nutmeg biscuits

175g (6 oz) cold butter, cubed
¾ cup caster (superfine) sugar
½ teaspoon vanilla extract
2 cups plain (all-purpose) flour
¼ cup (2 fl oz) honey
1 egg
honey icing
1½ cups icing (confectioner's) sugar, sifted
2 teaspoons honey
1–1½ tablespoons water
freshly grated nutmeg, for sprinkling

Place the butter, sugar and vanilla in the bowl of a food processor and process until smooth. Add the flour, honey and egg and process again to form a smooth dough. Knead the dough lightly, enclose in plastic wrap and refrigerate for 30 minutes. Preheat oven to 180°C (355°F). Roll tablespoons of the mixture into 4cm (1½ in) rounds and flatten slightly. Place the biscuits on baking trays lined with non-stick baking (parchment) paper. Bake the biscuits for 12–15 minutes or until dark golden. Cool on wire racks.

To make the honey icing, combine the icing sugar, honey and enough water until smooth and thick. Top the biscuits with the icing and sprinkle with the nutmeg. Store in an airtight container for up to a week. Makes 26.

chocolate christmas pudding

honey and nutmeg biscuits

simple menu: planning ahead

1 week before

- [ ] Order the pork from your butcher. When storing the pork in your refrigerator, keep it skin-side up so the skin stays dry, thereby ensuring a really crispy crackling.

- [ ] Make the honey and nutmeg biscuits and store in an airtight container.

- [ ] Marinate the olives and store in a sealed container in the refrigerator. Allow to stand at room temperature for 20 minutes before serving with drinks.

- [ ] Decide on and purchase the wines, aperitifs, beers and soft drinks to serve with your menu.

3 days before

- [ ] Make the mustard cream and store, covered, in the refrigerator.

2 days before

- [ ] Make the goat's cheese and dill quiches and store in an airtight container in the refrigerator. To reheat on the day, place on baking trays and cook at 180°C (355°F) for 8 minutes or until the quiches are warmed through.

- [ ] Make the chocolate christmas pudding, cool, cover and refrigerate. Warm in the microwave just before serving.

- [ ] Purchase all the fresh vegetables that are required for your menu.

1 day before

- [ ] Make the muffin stuffing and store in an airtight container in the refrigerator. Reheat uncovered in a 180°C (355°F) oven for 5 minutes before serving.

- [ ] Blanch the beans and broccolini for the salad, cover and refrigerate.

- [ ] Cook the pastry for the salmon and rocket tarts and store in an airtight container. Make the sour cream topping, cover and refrigerate until just before serving.

- [ ] Make the chocolate brandy sauce, cover and refrigerate. Warm in the microwave.

on the day

- [ ] Prepare the pork and place in the oven 1 hour 30 minutes before serving.

- [ ] Prepare the crunchy baby potatoes and place in the oven 40 minutes before serving.

- [ ] Assemble the salmon and rocket tarts.

- [ ] Make the balsamic dressing for the salad and warm the blanched vegetables in the dressing.

+ perfect pork

The secret to a crackling, crisp pork skin over tender, juicy meat is to begin the cooking process at a very high heat (200–220°C/390–425°F). Cook for 30 minutes or until the pork skin has bubbled and is crisp. Then reduce the temperature to 180°C (355°F) to cook the meat. Take care not to overcook or it will become dry and tough. There should still be some pink juices running through the meat.

sweet treats

Whether you're hosting a day of celebration, visiting
friends and family, or waiting for guests to drop by over the
holidays, a choice of festive little goodies will make their
day. The best thing about this selection is that you can
make them in advance so you'll be ready to join in the fun.
Serve your sweet treats with coffee, tea, hot chocolate
or eggnog... or wrap as a gift with the personal touch.

BISCUITS

*.

SLICES

*.

TARTS

*.

SWEETS

*.

PUDDINGS

berry almond tarts

almond truffle biscuits

fruit mince pies

berry almond tarts

90g (3 oz) butter, softened
¼ cup caster (superfine) sugar
1 egg
1 egg yolk, extra
1¼ cups almond meal (see glossary)
1½ tablespoons plain (all-purpose) flour
½ cup raspberries or blueberries
1 tablespoon icing (confectioner's) sugar

Preheat the oven to 150°C (300°F). Place the butter and sugar in the bowl of an electric mixer and beat until pale and creamy. Add the egg, egg yolk, almond meal and flour and beat until smooth. Grease 4 x 10cm (4 in) round tart tins and spoon in the mixture. Smooth the tops and sprinkle over the berries. Gently press the berries into the filling, sprinkle with the icing sugar and bake for 35–40 minutes or until golden. Store in an airtight container for up to 3 days. Makes 4.

almond truffle biscuits

55g (2 oz) unsalted butter, softened
½ cup (3½ oz) brown sugar
½ teaspoon vanilla extract
½ teaspoon finely grated orange rind
1 egg yolk
½ cup (2⅔ oz) plain (all-purpose) flour, sifted
¼ cup (1 oz) almond meal
¼ teaspoon baking powder
1 quantity chocolate truffle filling (recipe, page 76)

Preheat the oven to 160°C (320°F). Place the butter, sugar, vanilla and orange rind in the bowl of an electric mixer and beat for 8–10 minutes or until light and creamy. Add the egg and beat well to combine. Add the flour, almond meal and baking powder and beat for 1 minute or until well combined. Spoon 20 x ½ teaspoons onto a baking tray lined with non-stick baking (parchment) paper and flatten with your hand. Cook for 8–10 minutes or until golden. Allow to cool. Repeat with the remaining ingredients to make 66 biscuits. Place the chocolate truffle filling into a piping bag and pipe a small amount onto half the biscuits. Sandwich with the remaining biscuits. Makes 33.

fruit mince pies

700g (1½ lb) store-bought shortcrust pastry (or recipe, page 76)
1 egg, lightly beaten
caster (superfine) sugar, for sprinkling
fruit filling
1 large apple, peeled, cored and grated
⅓ cup sultanas
¼ cup candied peel
⅓ cup currants
⅓ cup slivered almonds
½ cup brown sugar
1 teaspoon mixed spice
30g (1 oz) butter, melted
2 tablespoons sherry

To prepare the fruit filling, place the apple, sultanas, candied peel, currants, almonds, sugar, mixed spice, butter and sherry in a bowl. Mix well, cover and refrigerate for 24 hours.

Preheat the oven to 180°C (355°F). Roll out the pastry until 2mm (⅛ in) thick. Cut into 7cm (2¾ in) rounds using a cookie cutter and place in shallow patty tins. Place 3 teaspoons of fruit mixture in each tart. Cut stars from the remaining pastry and place on top of the fruit mixture. Brush with the egg, sprinkle with the sugar and bake for 15 minutes or until golden. Store in an airtight container for up to 10 days. Makes 22.

simple shortbread

180g (6 oz) cold butter, chopped
¾ cup caster (superfine) sugar
1 cup cornflour (cornstarch), sifted
1½ cups plain (all-purpose) flour, sifted
1 egg

Preheat the oven to 160°C (320°F). Place the butter, sugar, cornflour, flour and egg in a food processor and process until smooth. Press the mixture into a shallow 20 x 30cm (8 x 12 in) tin lined with non-stick baking (parchment) paper. Score the top of the shortbread into bars. Bake for 35–40 minutes or until golden. Cool in the tin. Store in an airtight container for up to 1 week. Makes 16.

simple shortbread

sour cherry tarts

1 cup sour (morello) cherries, drained
2 tablespoons dessert wine
¼ cup sugar
1 egg
50g butter, melted
½ cup almond meal
2 sheets store-bought shortcrust pastry

Preheat the oven to 200°C (390°F). Combine the cherries and dessert wine, cover and set aside. Place the sugar and egg in a bowl and whisk until thickened. Add the butter and stir through the almond meal. Use an 8½cm (3 in) round cookie cutter to cut out six rounds of pastry. Push the pastry into six well greased ½ cup (4 fl oz) capacity muffin tins or tart tins. Spoon 2 teaspoons of the almond mixture into each tart and top with the cherry mixture. Bake for 20 minutes or until the tops are puffed and golden. Makes 6.

pistachio and cranberry nougat

2½ cups caster (superfine) sugar
1 cup (8 fl oz) liquid glucose
⅓ cup (2½ fl oz) honey
confectionery rice paper (see glossary)
2 egg whites
200g (7 oz) pistachio nuts, shelled
110g (4 oz) dried sweetened cranberries (see glossary)

Place the sugar, glucose and honey in a saucepan over medium heat and stir until the sugar begins to dissolve. Increase the heat and boil for 7 minutes or until 140°C (285°F) on a sugar (candy) thermometer.
   Line the base of a 20cm (8 in) square cake tin with rice paper. Place the egg whites in the bowl of an electric mixer and whisk until stiff peaks form. Add the sugar mixture in a thin, steady stream, beating constantly until the mixture is very thick. Fold in the pistachios and dried cranberries and spoon into the tin. Cover the nougat with rice paper and press to flatten. Set aside in a dry place for 8 hours or until set (do not refrigerate). To serve, remove the nougat from the tin and cut into squares. Store in a paper-lined airtight container away from moisture. Again, do not refrigerate. Makes 36 squares.

christmas muffins

2 cups plain (all-purpose) flour
2 teaspoons baking powder
1 teaspoon ground cinnamon
½ cup caster (superfine) sugar
300g (10½ oz) sour cream
1 egg
3 tablespoons vegetable oil
¾ cup dried sweetened cranberries (see glossary)
1 cup halved pitted cherries (fresh or from a jar)

Preheat the oven to 200°C (390°F). Place the flour, baking powder, cinnamon and sugar in a bowl and mix well. Place the sour cream, egg and oil in a bowl and whisk well. Add to the flour mixture with the cranberries and cherries and mix until just combined. Line 6 x 1 cup (8 fl oz) capacity ramekins with non-stick baking (parchment) paper, to make tall cylinders (see photo) and secure with string. Spoon the mixture into the ramekins and bake for 30 minutes or until cooked when tested with a skewer. Makes 6.

vanilla snap biscuits

185g (6½ oz) butter
1 cup caster (superfine) sugar
1½ teaspoons vanilla extract
2½ cups plain (all-purpose) flour
1 egg
1 egg yolk, extra
icing (confectioner's) sugar, to serve

Preheat the oven to 180°C (355°F). Process the butter, sugar and vanilla in a food processor until smooth. Add the flour, egg and extra yolk and process to form a dough. Knead lightly, wrap in plastic wrap and refrigerate for 30 minutes. Roll the dough between 2 sheets of non-stick baking (parchment) paper until 5mm (¼ in) thick. Use cookie cutters to cut into shapes. Place on baking trays lined with non-stick baking (parchment) paper. Bake for 10–12 minutes. Cool on wire racks and dust with icing sugar, if desired. Store in an airtight container for up to 1 week. Makes 45.

sour cherry tarts

christmas muffins

pistachio and cranberry nougat

vanilla snap biscuits

47

berry and brioche bake

brandy butter

panforte

berry and brioche bake

30g (1 oz) butter
1 tablespoon granulated sugar
1 brioche loaf (see glossary), cut into thick slices
500g (1 lb) strawberries, trimmed and halved
150g (5¼ oz) blueberries
⅓ cup (2½ fl oz) muscat
3 tablespoons caster (superfine) sugar

Preheat the oven to 180°C (355°F). Brush a 23 x 18cm (9 x 7 in) baking dish with the butter and sprinkle the granulated sugar over the base. Line the base with the brioche slices. Combine the strawberries, blueberries, muscat and caster sugar in a bowl. Spoon over the brioche and bake for 35 minutes or until the berries are soft and the brioche is golden. Serve warm or cold. Serves 8.

brandy butter

250g (8¾ oz) butter, softened
⅔ cup icing (confectioner's) sugar, sifted
2 tablespoons brandy
1 teaspoon vanilla extract

Beat the butter, icing sugar, brandy and vanilla extract in the bowl of an electric mixer for 7–10 minutes or until light and creamy. Store covered in the refrigerator for up to 1 week. Serve with warmed Christmas pudding (recipe, page 24). Serves 8.

panforte

1 cup toasted almonds, roughly chopped
¾ cup roasted hazelnuts, roughly chopped
1 cup chopped dried apricots
1½ cups (7⅞ oz) plain (all-purpose) flour, sifted
¼ cup (1 oz) cocoa powder, sifted
1 teaspoon cinnamon
¼ teaspoon allspice
1 cup (8 fl oz) honey
1 cup (7¾ oz) caster (superfine) sugar
confectionery rice paper, for lining (see glossary)

Preheat the oven to 180°C (350°F). Place the nuts, apricots, flour, cocoa, cinnamon and allspice in a large heatproof bowl. Place the honey and sugar in a saucepan and stir over a low heat until the sugar is dissolved. Brush the sides of the pan with a pastry brush dipped in water to remove any sugar crystals. Increase the heat and simmer for 1–2 minutes until "soft ball" stage (113–115°C/235–240°F on a sugar or candy thermometer). Pour into the flour mixture and stir quickly to combine. Line a 20 x 30cm (8 x 12 in) slice tin with sheets of rice paper and trim the edges. Press the mixture into the tin. Cook for 20 minutes or until springy. Cool in the tin. Cut into slices. Makes 24.

mini chocolate puddings

350g (12⅓ oz) store-bought Christmas pudding,
   roughly chopped
1 tablespoon brandy
200g (7 oz) dark cooking chocolate, melted
¼ cup cachous (silver decorating balls)

Place the pudding and brandy in a food processor and process in short bursts until it resembles fine breadcrumbs. Roll teaspoons of the mixture into small balls. Using a fork, dip the balls into the chocolate, place onto a baking tray lined with non-stick baking (parchment) paper and decorate each one with cachous. Allow to set at room temperature for 1 hour. Makes 30.

mini chocolate puddings

style + home

Create magical touches and special effects in every corner
of the house to capture the spirit of Christmas.

HOME DECORATION

candy cane cones ✳ greeting card chains
nostalgic settings

TABLE SETTINGS

bags of style ✳ floral centrepieces
good things in small packages

GIFTS FOR FOOD LOVERS

pie makings ✳ brunch for two
scoopfuls of sweets ✳ eggnog necessities

TREES WITH A TWIST

wood and cookies ✳ twig and tulle
sweet sensation

WRAPPED + TIED

in the bag ✳ spicy solutions
personalised papers

candy cane cones

Cut cardboard into 50cm (19½ in) diameter semicircles. Shape the
semicircles into cones, adhere the edges with double-sided tape then
punch holes for a wire or string handle. Fill the cones with candy
canes. Hang from the sides of mantlepieces or on door handles.

show your cards

A simple but effective way of showing off beautiful Christmas cards
is by hanging them around the house. Display your season's greetings
by tying lengths of ribbon to an adhesive hook or curtain rail and
securing the cards with paper clips, small pegs or coloured pins.

Christmas past

Adorn the mantelpiece of a faux fireplace or bookshelf with stockings
and ornaments that have been collected through the years. Unify the
arrangement by using similar colours and textures and tie them to an
artificial blossom branch or a simple branch from your garden.

bag of tricks

White paper bags trimmed with a zigzag edge, using pinking shears, and tied to the backs of chairs with red ribbon or cord make inventive placecards. You could write your guests' names on the bags and fill each one with a sweet take-home, or after Christmas dinner, surprise.

unifying statement

A ceramic dish filled with flowers is a simple way to pull together your colour scheme. Trim the stems and slot the blooms through a cake cooler or baking rack for an easy way of keeping the flowers tightly grouped together for a low centrepiece on the festive table.

DINNER

...lade Glazed Ham

...Onion Relish

...amed Butter Beans

Honey Carrots

Parmesan Potatoes

Individual Christmas Puddings

small packages

For a personal touch at the table, create a place card that doubles
duty as a take-home treat. Wrap mini plum puddings, truffles or
chocolate-coated pudding balls (make your own using the recipe on
page 50) in unbleached calico and tie on tags with red string or wool.

easy as pie

By staying away from fresh food, you can put together hampers in advance. The pie-maker in your life will love a rolling pin, crimp cutter, pastry brush, pie dish and ceramic pastry weights. Use a tea towel as a base and secure all the components together with ribbon or braid.

a sparkling start

Christmas brunch for two? Get the big day off to a good start by preparing a gift to share with someone special. Sparkling water, mini Champagnes, peach nectar (so you can make Bellinis) and brioche (or the Christmas muffins on page 46) fit neatly in a bottle carrier.

sweet treats

For a sparkling sideboard decoration, fill glass jars, bowls and tumblers with jelly beans, sugared almonds, silver-dipped sweets, marshmallows and mints. Leave out a scoop and paper bags for an old-fashioned sweet shop feel. Children, big and small, will love it.

winter warmers

Put together the makings for the traditional Christmas tipple. In a mixing bowl, present a milk heating pan, ceramic cups, nutmeg grater, small whisk, whole nutmeg, vanilla bean pods and a miniature bottle of brandy or rum to make it simple to prepare the perfect eggnog.

wood + cookies

Tie bundles of timber or driftwood together and attach to a central post with rope. Secure the tree in a bucket filled with white pebbles. Attach Christmas bauble-shaped cookies decorated with icing and sugar sprinkles. Have extras on hand for those who can't resist a sample.

twig + tulle

A winter tree branch can become a strikingly simple and sophisticated centrepiece for your room. Tie short lengths of white tulle, ribbon or metallic fabric to the branch and anchor it in a glass vase that has been filled with sand to keep the tree from toppling over.

sweet sensation

Nail lengths of wood to a central post then water down some white
paint to create a whitewashed effect. Place in a ceramic pot filled with
white pebbles, then decorate with biscuits, chocolates or sweets that
are wrapped in your colour theme and tied to the wood with string.

61

in the bag

Paper bags of all colours and sizes are available from stationers, or try department stores for cloth bags and pouches. You can also search fabric shops for remnants, which are usually very cheap. Seal with a sticky label, safety or hat pin, or go crafty by sewing on a button.

touch of spice

Capture the heady scents of Christmas by adding sticks of cinnamon and star anise to finish off your gifts. Wrap gifts in cross stitch linen or tie boxes with cross stitch ribbon, or ribbon in contrasting colours. Traditional red and white works well, or perhaps a green contrast.

custom wrapped

Choose your wrapping paper to suit the gift's recipient. Try the financial
pages for the investor, sheet music for the song buff, or poetry for a hint
of romance. Paper dressmaking patterns might appeal to the sewer in
your circle. Offset the practical paper by selecting pretty trimmings.

choir of angels

These festive cookies are made using the vanilla snap biscuit recipe on page 46. Insert holes for ribbon with a skewer before baking. When completely cooled, string the angels together for a festive garland that's great for decorating the mantelpiece, window sill or bookshelf.

christmas keepsake

Keep a record of your festivities… note down your recipes,

add a few family favourites and make sure this Christmas

is one you'll remember for years to come.

*.

our christmas _____ year _____

location _____

guest list _____

_____   _____

_____   _____

_____   _____

_____   _____

_____   _____

_____   _____

_____   _____

recipes cooked _____

_____   _____

_____   _____

_____   _____

_____   _____

_____   _____

_____   _____

_____   _____

_____   _____

wines served _____

_____   _____

_____   _____

_____   _____

_____   _____

_____   _____

our christmas _____ year _____

location _____

guest list _____

_____   _____

_____   _____

_____   _____

_____   _____

_____   _____

_____   _____

_____   _____

recipes cooked _____

_____   _____

_____   _____

_____   _____

_____   _____

_____   _____

_____   _____

_____   _____

wines served _____

_____   _____

_____   _____

_____   _____

_____   _____

our christmas _____ year _____

location _____

guest list _____

_____ _____

_____ _____

_____ _____

_____ _____

_____ _____

_____ _____

_____ _____

recipes cooked _____

_____ _____

_____ _____

_____ _____

_____ _____

_____ _____

_____ _____

_____ _____

wines served _____

_____ _____

_____ _____

_____ _____

_____ _____

our christmas _____ year _____

location _____

guest list _____

_____   _____

_____   _____

_____   _____

_____   _____

_____   _____

_____   _____

_____   _____

recipes cooked _____

_____   _____

_____   _____

_____   _____

_____   _____

_____   _____

_____   _____

_____   _____

_____   _____

wines served _____

_____   _____

_____   _____

_____   _____

_____   _____

_____   _____

our christmas _____ year _____

location _____

guest list _____

_____   _____

_____   _____

_____   _____

_____   _____

_____   _____

_____   _____

_____   _____

recipes cooked _____

_____   _____

_____   _____

_____   _____

_____   _____

_____   _____

_____   _____

_____   _____

_____   _____

wines served _____

_____   _____

_____   _____

_____   _____

_____   _____

our christmas _____ year _____

location _____

guest list _____

_____ _____

_____ _____

_____ _____

_____ _____

_____ _____

_____ _____

_____ _____

_____ _____

recipes cooked _____

_____ _____

_____ _____

_____ _____

_____ _____

_____ _____

_____ _____

_____ _____

_____ _____

wines served _____

_____ _____

_____ _____

_____ _____

_____ _____

our christmas _____ year _____

location _____

guest list _____

_____   _____

_____   _____

_____   _____

_____   _____

_____   _____

_____   _____

_____   _____

recipes cooked _____

_____   _____

_____   _____

_____   _____

_____   _____

_____   _____

_____   _____

_____   _____

_____   _____

wines served _____

_____   _____

_____   _____

_____   _____

_____   _____

our christmas _____ year _____

location _____

guest list _____ . _____

_____ _____

_____ _____

_____ _____

_____ _____

_____ _____

_____ _____

_____ _____

recipes cooked _____

_____ _____

_____ _____

_____ _____

_____ _____

_____ _____

_____ _____

_____ _____

wines served _____

_____ _____

_____ _____

_____ _____

_____ _____

notes

notes

almond meal

A richer alternative to flour made from ground almonds. Primarily for cakes and desserts but can also be used to thicken sauces or coat meat and fish for frying.

brioche

A sweet French bread made in a loaf or bun. Traditionally dunked in coffee at breakfast. Available from speciality bread stores and some supermarkets.

calico cloth

An inexpensive, unbleached natural fabric available at home furnishing stores and in haberdashery departments. It is tough enough to withstand the boiling process and won't shrink.

capers

The small, green flower buds of the caper bush. Available packed in brine or salt. Use salt-packed capers when possible, as the texture is firmer and the flavour superior. Rinse thoroughly before use.

chocolate truffle filling

Place 200g (7 oz) dark cooking chocolate, ¼ cup (2 fl oz) (single or pouring) cream and 20g (¾ oz) unsalted butter in a small saucepan over low heat and stir until the chocolate is melted and smooth. Set aside and allow to cool for 30 minutes.

cranberries, dried

Sweetened to reduce their tart flavour and perfect for baking and confectionery. Available from the dried fruit section of large supermarkets and health food stores.

rice paper (confectionery)

A translucent, edible paper sometimes callled wafer paper made from water and the pith of various starchy plants. Flavourless, it can be used to wrap nougat or line patty tins and eaten along with the cakes or confectionery.

risotto, basic

Place 6 cups (48 fl oz) chicken stock in a pan over medium heat. Cover and bring to a simmer. Heat a large pan over medium heat, add 20g (¾ oz) butter, 1 tablespoon olive oil and 1 chopped brown onion and cook for 6 minutes or until soft and golden. Add 2 cups arborio rice to the onion mixture, stirring for 2 minutes or until the grains are translucent and coated. Add the hot stock to the rice 1 cup (8 fl oz) at a time, stirring continuously until each cup of stock is absorbed and the rice is al dente (around 25–30 minutes). Stir through ½ cup grated parmesan cheese, 20g (¾ oz) butter, sea salt and cracked black pepper. Serves 4.

scoring

A method of preparation that involves running the point of a knife over the surface of meat or seafood in a cross-hatch formation so that it cuts about halfway through. Commonly used when preparing leg ham for glazing or pork for roasting.

pastry

Make your own or use one of the many store-bought varieties.

puff pastry

This pastry is time-consuming and quite difficult to make, so many cooks opt to use store-bought puff pastry. It can be bought in blocks from patisseries or bought in both block and sheet forms from the supermarket. You may need to layer several sheets together to make the desired thickness.

shortcrust pastry

A savoury or sweet pastry that is available ready-made in blocks and frozen sheets. Keep a supply in the freezer for last-minute pies and desserts or make your own.

shortcrust pastry recipe

Process 2 cups plain (all-purpose) flour with 145g (5 oz) butter in a food processor until the mixture resembles fine breadcrumbs. With the motor running, add enough iced water to form a dough. Knead lightly then wrap in plastic wrap and refrigerate for 30 minutes. Roll to 2mm (⅛ in) thick. Makes 350g (12 oz).

vanilla bean

The pod of an orchid vine native to Central America. It is added, either whole or split, to hot milk or cream to allow the flavour to infuse. Available from specialty food stores, supermarkets and delicatessens. Store the beans in an airtight container.

conversion chart

Used throughout this book:
1 Australian tablespoon = 20ml (4 teaspoons)

1 teaspoon = 5ml
1 UK tablespoon = 15ml (3 teaspoons/½ fl oz)
1 cup = 250ml (8 fl oz)

liquid conversions

metric	imperial	cups
30ml	1 fl oz	⅛ cup
60ml	2 fl oz	¼ cup
80ml	2¾ fl oz	⅓ cup
125ml	4 fl oz	½ cup
185ml	6 fl oz	¾ cup
250ml	8 fl oz	1 cup
375ml	12 fl oz	1½ cups
500ml	16 fl oz	2 cups
600ml	20 fl oz	2½ cups
750ml	24 fl oz	3 cups
1 litre	32 fl oz	4 cups

cup measures

1 cup almond meal	110g	3½ oz
1 cup breadcrumbs, fresh	50g	2 oz
1 cup sugar, brown	200g	6½ oz
1 cup sugar, white	225g	7 oz
1 cup caster (superfine) sugar	225g	7 oz
1 cup icing (confectioner's) sugar	125g	4 oz
1 cup plain (all-purpose) flour	125g	4 oz
1 cup rice flour	100g	3½ oz
1 cup rice, cooked	165g	5½ oz
1 cup arborio rice, uncooked	220g	7 oz
1 cup couscous, uncooked	180g	6 oz
1 cup basil leaves	45g	1½ oz
1 cup coriander (cilantro) leaves	40g	1¼ oz
1 cup mint leaves	35g	1¼ oz
1 cup flat-leaf parsley leaves	40g	1¼ oz
1 cup cashews, whole	150g	5 oz
1 cup cooked chicken, shredded	150g	5 oz
1 cup olives	175g	6 oz
1 cup parmesan cheese, finely grated	100g	3½ oz
1 cup green peas, frozen	170g	5½ oz

donna hay is an Australian-based food stylist, author and magazine editor and one of the best-known names in cookbook and magazine publishing in the world. Her previous thirteen books have sold more than 3.3 million copies internationally and are renowned for their fresh style, easy-to-follow recipes and inspirational photography. These best-selling, award-winning titles – including *instant entertaining, the instant cook, modern classics book 1, modern classics book 2* and *off the shelf* – together with *donna hay magazine* have captured the imagination of cooks worldwide and set a new benchmark in modern food styling and publishing.